S0-BHZ-420

Holiness:

The False and the True

by

Harry A. Ironside

www.harryironsidebooks.com

www.solidchristianbooks.com

CORRECTIONS ARE MADE BY COMPARING TO THE ORIGINAL BOOK.

Contents

INSERT
4
COLOR PAGES
HERE

Introduction

It is my desire, in dependence on the Lord, to write a faithful record, so far as memory now serves me, of some of God's dealings with my soul and my strivings after the experience of holiness, during the first six years of my Christian life, ere I knew the blessedness of finding all in Christ. This will make it necessary at times, I have little doubt, to "speak as a fool"--even as the apostle Paul did: but as I reflect on the need for such a record, I think I can say with him, "Ye have compelled me."

If I may be privileged to thereby save others from the unhappy experiences I passed through in those early years, I shall feel abundantly repaid for the effort it will take to thus put these heart-experiences before my readers.

From a very early age God began to speak to me through His Word. I doubt if I could go back to the first time when, to my recollection, I felt something of the reality of eternal things.

My father was taken from me ere his features were impressed upon my infant mind. But I never have heard him spoken of other than as a man of God. He was known in Toronto (my birthplace) to many as "The Eternity Man." His Bible, marked in many places, was a precious legacy to me; and from it I learned to recite my first verse of Scripture, at the age of four. I distinctly recall learning the blessed words of Luke 19:10, "For the Son of man is come to seek and to save that which was lost." That I was lost, and that Christ Jesus came from heaven to save me, were the first divine truths impressed on my young heart.

My widowed mother was, it seems to me, one of a thousand. I remember yet how I would be thrilled as she knelt with me as a child, and prayed, "O Father, keep my boy from ever desiring anything greater than to live for Thee. Save him early, and make him a devoted street-preacher, as his father was. Make him willing to suffer for Jesus' sake, to gladly endure persecution and rejection by the world that cast out Thy Son; and keep him from what would dishonor Thee." The words were not always the same, but I have heard the sentiment times without number.

To our home there often came servants of Christ--plain, godly men, who seemed to me to carry with them the atmosphere of eternity. Yet in a very real sense they were the bane of my boyhood. Their searching, "Henry, lad, are you born again yet?" or the equally impressive, "Are you certain that your soul is saved?" often brought me to a standstill; but I knew not how to reply.

California had become my home ere I was clear as to being a child of God. In Los Angeles I first began to learn the love of the world, and was impatient of restraint. Yet I had almost continual concern as to the great matter of my salvation.

I was but twelve years old when I began a Sunday-school and set up to try to help the boys and girls of the neighborhood to a knowledge of the Book I had read ten times through, but which had still left me without assurance of salvation.

To Timothy, Paul wrote, "From a child thou hast known the Holy Scriptures, which are able to make thee wise unto salvation, through faith which is in Christ Jesus" (2 Tim. 3:15). It was this latter that I lacked. I had, it seemed to me, always believed, yet I dared not say I was saved. I know now that I had always believed about Jesus. I had not really believed in Him as my personal Saviour. Between the two there is all the difference that there is between being saved and lost, between an eternity in Heaven and endless ages in the lake of fire.

As I have said, I was not without considerable anxiety as to my soul; and though I longed to break into the world, and was indeed guilty of much that was vile and wicked, I ever felt a restraining hand upon me, keeping me from many things that I would otherwise have gone into; and a certain religiousness became, I suppose, characteristic. But religion is not salvation.

I was nearly fourteen years old when, upon returning one day from school, I learned that a servant of Christ from Canada, well known to me, had arrived for meetings. I knew, ere I saw him, how he would greet me; for I remembered him well, and his searching questions, when I was younger. Therefore I was not surprised, but embarrassed nevertheless, when he exclaimed, "Well, Harry, lad, I'm glad to see you. And are you born again yet?"

The blood mantled my face; I hung my head, and could find no words to reply. An uncle present said, "You know, Mr. M--, he preaches himself now a bit, and conducts a Sunday School!"

"Indeed!" was the answer. "Will you get your Bible, Harry?"

I was glad to get out of the room, and so went at once for my Bible, and returned, after remaining out ~~of the room~~ as long as seemed decent, hoping thereby to recover myself. Upon my re-entering the room, he said, kindly, but seriously, "Will you turn to Rom. 3:19, and read it aloud?"

Slowly I read, "Now we know that what things soever the law saith, it saith to them who are under the law: that every mouth may be stopped, and all the world may become guilty before God." I felt the application, and was at a loss for words. The evangelist went on to tell me that he too had been once a religious sinner, till God stopped his mouth, and then gave him a sight of Christ. He pressed on me the importance of getting to the same place ere I tried to teach others.

The words had their effect. From that time till I was sure I was saved, I refrained from talking of these things, and I gave up my Sunday-school work. But now Satan, who was seeking my soul's destruction, suggested to me, "If lost and unfit to speak of religious things to others, why not enjoy all the world has to offer, so far as you are able to avail yourself of it?"

I listened only too eagerly to his words, and for the next six months or thereabouts no one was more anxious for folly than I, though always with a smarting conscience.

At last, on a Thursday evening in February 1890, God spoke to me in tremendous power while out at a party with a lot of other young people, mostly older than myself, intent only on an evening's amusement. I remember now that I had withdrawn from the parlor for a few moments to obtain a cooling drink in the next room. Standing alone at the refreshment table, there came home to my inmost soul, in startling clearness, some verses of Scripture I had learned months before. They are found in the first chapter of Proverbs, beginning with verse 24 and going on to verse 32. Here wisdom is represented as laughing at the calamity of the one who refused to heed instruction, and mocking when his fear cometh. Every word seemed to burn its way into my heart. I saw as never before my dreadful guilt in having so long refused to trust Christ for myself, and in having preferred my own wilful way to that of Him who had died for me.

I went back to the parlor, and tried to join with the rest in their empty follies. But all seemed utterly hollow, and the tinsel was gone. The light of eternity was shining into the room, and I wondered how any could laugh with God's judgment hanging over us, like a Damocles' sword suspended by a hair. We seemed like people sporting with closed eyes on the edge of a precipice, and I the most careless of all, till grace had made me see.

That night, when all was over, I hurried home, and crept up-stairs to my room. There, after lighting a lamp, I took my Bible, and, with it before me, fell upon my knees.

I had an undefined feeling that I had better pray. But the thought came, "What shall I pray for?" Clearly and distinctly came back the answer, "For what God has been offering me for years. Why not then receive it, and thank Him?"

My dear mother had often said, "The place to begin with God is Romans 3, or John 3." To both these scriptures I turned, and read them carefully. Clearly I saw that I was a helpless sinner, but that Christ for me had died, and that salvation was offered freely to all who trusted in Him. Reading John 3:16 the second time, I said, "That will do. O God, I thank Thee that Thou has loved me, and given Thy Son for me. I trust Him now as my Saviour, and I rest on Thy Word, which tells me I have everlasting life."

Then I expected to feel a thrill of joy. It did not come. I wondered if I could be mistaken. I expected a sudden rush of love for Christ. It did not come either. I feared I could not be really saved with so little emotion.

I read the words again. There could be no mistake. God loved the world, of which I formed a part. God gave His Son to save all believers. I believed in Him as my Saviour. Therefore I must have everlasting life. Again I thanked Him, and rose from my knees to begin the walk of faith. God could not lie. I knew I must be saved.

Holiness: The Great Desideratum

Being saved myself, the first great desires that sprang up in my heart was an intense longing to lead others to the One who had made my peace with God.

At the time of which I write, the Salvation Army was in the zenith of its energy as an organization devoted to going out after the lost. It had not yet become popular, a society to be patronized by the world and used as a medium for philanthropic work. Its officers and soldiers seemed to have but one aim and object--to lead the weary and despairing to the Saviour's feet. I had often attended its services, and in fact had frequently, though but a child, given a "testimony" by quoting Scripture and urging sinners to trust Christ, even while I was in the dark myself. Naturally therefore, when the knowledge of salvation was mine, I went at the first opportunity, the night after my conversion, to an "Army" street-meeting, and there spoke for the first time, in the open air, of the grace of God so newly revealed to my soul.

I suppose, because I was but a lad of fourteen and fairly familiar with the Bible, and also somewhat forward-- unduly so, I have little doubt--I was at once cordially welcomed among them, and soon became known as "the boy preacher," a title which, I fear, ministered more to the pride of my heart than I had any idea of at the time. For, in fact, in my new-found joy I had no conception that I still carried about with me a nature as sinful and vile as existed in the breast of the greatest evildoer in the world. I knew something of Christ and His love; I knew little or nothing of myself and the deceitfulness of my own heart.

As nearly as I can now recollect, I was in the enjoyment of the knowledge of God's salvation about a month when, in some dispute with my brother, who was younger than I, my temper suddenly escaped control, and in an angry passion I struck and felled him to the ground. Horror immediately filled my soul. I needed not his sarcastic taunt, "Well, you are a nice Christian! You'd better go down to the Army and tell what a saint you've become!" to send me to my room in anguish of heart to confess my sin to God in shame and bitter sorrow, as afterwards frankly to my brother, who generously forgave me.

From this time on mine was an "up-and-down experience," to use a term often heard in "testimony meetings." I longed for perfect victory over the lusts and desires of the flesh. Yet I seemed to have more trouble with evil thoughts and unholy propensities than I had ever known before. For a long time I kept these conflicts hidden, and known only to God and to myself. But after some eight or ten months, I became interested in what were called "holiness meetings," held weekly in the "Army" hall, and also in a mission I sometimes attended.

At these gatherings an experience was spoken of which I felt was just what I needed. It was designated by various terms: "The Second Blessing"; "Sanctification"; "Perfect Love"; "Higher Life"; "Cleansing from Inbred Sin"; and by other expressions.

Substantially, the teaching was this: When converted, God graciously forgives all sins committed up to the time when one repents. But the believer is then placed in a lifelong probation, during which he may at any time forfeit his justification and peace with God if he falls into sin from which he does not AT ONCE repent. In order, therefore, to maintain himself in a saved condition, he needs a further work of grace called sanctification. This work has to do with sin the root, as justification had to do with sins the fruit.

The steps leading up to this second blessing are, firstly, conviction as to the need of holiness (just as in the beginning there was conviction of the need of salvation); secondly, a full surrender to God, or the laying of every hope, prospect and possession on the altar of consecration; thirdly, to claim in faith the incoming of the Holy Spirit as a refining fire to burn out all inbred sin, thus destroying IN TOTO every lust and passion, leaving the soul perfect in love and as pure as unfallen Adam.

This wonderful blessing received, great watchfulness is required lest, as the serpent beguiled Eve, he deceive the sanctified soul, and thus introduce again the same kind of an evil principle which called for such drastic action before.

Such was the teaching; and coupled with it were heartfelt testimonies of experiences so remarkable that I could not doubt THEIR genuineness, nor that what others seemed to enjoy was likewise for me if I would fulfil the conditions.

One AGED lady told how for forty years she had been kept from sin in thought, word, and deed. Her heart, she declared, was no longer "deceitful above all things, and desperately wicked," but was as holy as the courts of heaven, since the blood of Christ has washed away the last remains OF inbred sin. Others spoke in a similar way, though their

11

experiences were much briefer. Bad tempers had been rooted out when a full surrender was made.

Evil propensities and unholy appetites had been instantly destroyed when holiness was claimed by faith.

Eagerly I began to seek this precious boon of holiness in the flesh. Earnestly I prayed for this Adamic sinlessness. I asked God to reveal to me every unholy thing, that I might truly surrender all to Him. I gave up friends, pursuits, pleasures--everything I could think of that might hinder the incoming of the Holy Ghost and the consequent blessing. I was a veritable "book-worm," an intense love for literature possessing me from childhood; but in my ignorant desire I put away all books of pleasurable or instructive character, and promised God to read only the Bible and holiness writings if He would only give me "the blessing." I did not, however, obtain what I sought, though I prayed zealously for weeks.

At last, one Saturday night (I was Now away from home, living with a friend, a member of the "Army"), I determined to go out into the country and wait on God, not returning till I had received the blessing of perfect love. I took a train at eleven o'clock, and went to a lonely station twelve miles from Los Angeles. There I alighted, and, leaving the highway, descended into an empty arroyo, or water-course. Falling on my knees beneath a sycamore tree, I prayed in an agony for hours, beseeching God to show me anything that hindered my reception of the blessing. Various matters of too private and sacred a nature to be here related came to my mind. I struggled against conviction, but finally ended by crying, "Lord, I give up all--everything, every person, every enjoyment,

12

that would hinder my living alone for Thee. Now give me, I pray Thee, the blessing!"

As I look back, I believe I was fully surrendered to the will of God at that moment, so far as I understood it. But my brain and nerves were unstrung by the long midnight vigil and the intense anxiety of previous months, and I fell almost fainting to the ground. Then a holy ecstasy seemed to thrill all my being. This I thought was the coming into my heart of the Comforter. I cried out in confidence, "Lord, I believe Thou dost come in. Thou dost cleanse and purify me from all sin. I claim it now. The work is done. I am sanctified by Thy blood. Thou dost make me holy. I believe; I believe!" I was unspeakably happy. I felt that all my struggles were ended.

With a heart filled with praise, I rose from the ground and began to sing aloud. Consulting my watch, I saw it was about half-past three in the morning. I felt I must hasten to town so as to be in time for the seven o'clock prayer-meeting, there to testify to my experience. Fatigued as I was by being up all night, yet so light was my heart I scarcely noticed the long miles back, but hastened to the city, arriving just as the meeting was beginning, buoyed up by my new-found experience. All were rejoiced as I told what great things I believed God had done for me. Every meeting that day added to my gladness. I was literally intoxicated with joyous emotions.

My troubles were all ended now. The wilderness was past, and I was in Canaan, feeding on the old corn of the land. Nevermore should I be troubled by inward drawings toward sin. My heart was pure. I had reached the desirable state of full sanctification. With no foe within, I could direct all my energies toward vanquishing the enemies without.

This was what I thought. Alas, how little did I know myself; much less the mind of God!

Sunshine and Clouds

For some weeks after the eventful experience before described, I lived in a dreamily-happy state, rejoicing in my fancied sinlessness. One great idea had possession of my mind; and whether at work or in my leisure hours, I thought of little else than the wonderful event which had taken place. But gradually I began to "come back to earth," as it were. I was now employed in a photographic studio, where I associated with people of various tastes and habits, some of whom ridiculed, some tolerated, and others sympathized with, my radical views on things religious.

Night after night I attended the meetings, speaking on the street and indoors, and I soon noticed (and doubtless others did too) that a change came over my "testimonies." Before, I had always held up Christ, and pointed the lost to Him. Now, almost imperceptibly, my own experience became my theme, and I held up myself as a striking example of consecration and holiness! This was the prevailing characteristic of the brief addresses made by most of the "advanced" Christians in our company. The youngest in grace magnified Christ. The "sanctified" magnified themselves. A favorite song will make this more manifest than any words of mine. It is still widely used in Army meetings, and finds a place in their song or hymnbooks. I give only one verse as a specimen:

> The people I know don't live holy;
> They battle with unconquered sin,
> Not daring to consecrate fully,
> Or they full salvation would win.

With malice they have constant trouble,
From doubting they long to be free;
With most things about them they grumble;
Praise God, this is not so with ME!

Will the reader believe me when I say that I sang this wretched doggerel without a thought of the sinful pride to which it was giving expression? I considered it my duty to continually direct attention to "my experience of full salvation," as it was called. "If you don't testify to it, you will lose the blessing," was accepted as an axiom among us.

As time went on, I began to be again conscious of inward desires toward evil – of thoughts that were unholy. I was nonplused. Going to a leading teacher for help, he said, "These are but temptations. Temptation is not sin. You only sin if you yield to the evil suggestion." This gave me peace for a time. I found it was the general way of excusing such evident movings of a fallen nature, which was supposed to have been eliminated. But gradually I sank to a lower and lower place, permitting things I would once have shunned; and I even observed that all about me did the same. The first ecstatic experiences seldom lasted long. The ecstasy departed, and the "sanctified" were very little different from their brethren who were supposed to be "only justified." We did not commit overt acts of evil: therefore we were sinless. Lust was not sin unless yielded to: so it was easy to go on testifying that all was right.

I purposely pass briefly over the next four years. In the main they were seasons of ignorantly happy service. I was young in years and in grace. My thoughts of sin, as well as of holiness, were very unformed and imperfect.

Therefore it was easy, generally speaking, to think that I was living without the one, and manifesting the other. When doubts assailed, I treated them as temptations of the devil. If I became unmistakably conscious that I had actually sinned, I persuaded myself that at least it was not willful, but rather a mistake of the mind than an intentional error of the heart. Then I went to God in confession, and prayed to be cleansed from secret faults.

When but sixteen years of age I became a cadet; that is, a student preparing for officership in the Salvation Army. During my probation in the Oakland Training Garrison I had more trouble than at any other time. The rigorous discipline and enforced intimate association with young men of so various tastes and tendencies, as also degrees of spiritual experience, was very hard on one of my supersensitive temperament. I saw very little holiness there, and I fear I exhibited much less. In fact, for the last two out of my five months' term I was all at sea, and dared not profess sanctification at all, owing to my low state. I was tormented with the thought that I had backslidden, and might be lost eternally after all my former happy experiences of the Lord's goodness. Twice I slipped out of the building when all were in bed, and made my way to a lonely spot where I spent the night in prayer, beseeching God not to take His Holy Spirit from me, but to again cleanse me fully from all inbred sin. Each time I "claimed it by faith," and was brighter for a few weeks; but I inevitably again fell into doubt and gloom, and was conscious of sinning both in thought and in word, and sometimes in unholy actions, which brought terrible remorse.

Finally, I was commissioned as lieutenant. Again I spent the night in prayer, feeling that I must not go out to teach and lead others unless myself pure and holy. Buoyed up with the thought of being free from the restraint I had been subjected to so long, it was comparatively easy this time to believe that the work of full inward cleansing was indeed consummated, and that I was now, if never before, actually rid of all carnality.

How readily one yields himself to self-deception in a matter of this kind! From this time on I became a more earnest advocate of the second blessing than ever; and I remember that often I prayed God to give my dear mother the blessing He had given me, and to make her as holy as her son had become. And that pious mother had known Christ before I was born, and knew her own heart too well to talk of sinlessness, though living a devoted, Christlike life!

As lieutenant for a year, and then as captain, I thoroughly enjoyed my work, gladly enduring hardship and privation that I fear I would shrink from now; generally confident that I was living out the doctrine of perfect love to God and man, and thereby making my own final salvation more secure. [Note: Perhaps I ought to explain for the benefit of the uninitiated that a "captain" has charge of a corps, or mission. A "lieutenant" assists a "captain."] And yet, as I now look back, what grave failures I can detect--what an unsubdued will--what lightness and frivolity--what lack of subjection to the word of God--what self-satisfaction and complacency! Alas, "man at his best estate is altogether vanity."

I was between eighteen and nineteen years of age when I began to entertain serious doubts as to my actually having attained so high a standard of Christian living as I had professed, and as the Army and other Holiness movements advocated as the only real Christianity. What led to this was of too personal and private a nature to publish; but it resulted in struggle and efforts toward self-crucifixion that brought disappointment and sorrow of a most poignant character; but it showed me beyond a doubt that the doctrine of death to nature was a miserable sophism, and that the carnal mind was still a part of my being.

Nearly eighteen months of an almost constant struggle followed. In vain I searched my heart to see if I had made a full surrender, and tried to give up every known thing that seemed in any sense evil or doubtful. Sometimes, for a month at a time, or even longer, I could persuade myself that at last I had indeed again received the blessing. But invariably a few weeks would bring before me once more that which proved that it was in my particular case all a delusion.

I did not dare open my heart to my assistants in the work, or to the "soldiers" who were under my guidance. To do so I felt would be to lose all influence with them and to be looked upon as a backslider. So, alone and in secret, I fought my battles and never went into a holiness meeting without persuading myself that now at least, I was fully surrendered and therefore must have the blessing of sanctification. Sometimes I called it entire consecration and felt easier. It did not seem to be claiming too much. I had no conception at the time of the hypocrisy of all this.

What made my distress more poignant was the knowledge that I was not the only sufferer. Another, one very dear to me, shared my doubts and anxieties from the same cause. For that other it eventually meant utter shipwreck of the faith; and one of the loveliest souls I ever knew was lost in the mazes of spiritualism. God grant it may not be forever, but that mercy may be found of the Lord in that day!

And now I began to see what a string of derelicts this holiness teaching left in its train. I could count scores of persons who had gone into utter infidelity because of it. They always gave the same reason: "I tried it all. I found it a failure. So I concluded the Bible teaching was all a delusion, and religion was a mere matter of the emotions." Many more (and I knew several such intimately) lapsed into insanity after floundering in the morass of this emotional religion for years--and people said that studying the Bible had driven them crazy. How little they knew that it was lack of Bible knowledge that was accountable for their wretched mental state--an absolutely unscriptural use of isolated passages of Scripture!

At last I became so troubled I could not go on with my work. I concluded to resign from the Salvation Army, and did so, but was persuaded by the colonel (note: answering to a bishop in some other denominations.) to wait six months ere the resignation took effect. At his suggestion I gave up corps work and went out on a special tour--where I did not need to touch the holiness question. But I preached to others many times when I was tormented by the thought that I might myself be finally lost, because, "without holiness no man shall see the Lord"; and, try as I would, I could not be sure I possessed it. I talked with any who seemed to me to really have the blessing I craved; but there were very few who, upon an intimate acquaintanceship, seemed genuine. I observed that the general state of "sanctified" people was as low, if not often lower, than that of those whom they contemptuously described as "only justified."

Finally, I could bear it no longer, so asked to be relieved from all active service, and at my own request was sent to the Beulah Home of Rest, near Oakland.

It was certainly time; for five years' active work, with only two brief furloughs, had left me almost a nervous wreck, worn out in body and most acutely distressed in mind.

The language of my troubled soul, after all those years of preaching to others, was, "Oh that I knew where I might find Him!" Finding Him not, I saw only the blackness of despair before me; but yet I knew too well His love and care to be completely cast down.

The Struggle Ended

I had now been for over five years laboring in the organization with which I had linked myself, and ever seeking to be certain that I had attained a sinless state. In some twelve different towns and cities I had served, as I thought, faithfully, endeavoring to reach the lost, and to make out of them staunch Salvationists when converted. Many happy experiences had been mine, coupled, however, with some most gloomy disappointments, both as to myself and others. Very few of our "converts" stood. "Backsliders" often outnumbered by far our "soldiers." The ex-Salvation Army was many times larger than the original organization.

One great reason for this I was blind to for a long time. But at last it began to be clear to me that the holiness doctrine had a most baneful influence upon the movement. People who professed conversion (whether real or not the day will declare) struggled for months, even years, to reach a state of sinlessness which never was reached; and at last they gave up in despair and sank back in many instances to the dead level of the world around them.

I saw that it was the same with all the holiness denominations, and the various "Bands," "Missions," and other movements, that were continually breaking off from them. The standard set was the unattainable. The result was, sooner or later, utter discouragement, cunningly-concealed hypocrisy, or an unconscious lowering of the standard to suit the experience reached. For myself, I had been ensnared by that last expedient for a long time. How much of the second there was I do not dare to say. But eventually I fell a victim to the first. And I can now see that it was a mercy I did so.

When I went to the Home of Rest, I had not yet fully given up seeking for perfection in the flesh. I really expected great things from the six months' furlough granted me, in order to "find myself," as it were.

Closely allied to the Home were other institutions where holiness and faith-healing were largely dwelt upon. I felt sure that in so hallowed an atmosphere great things would be accomplished.

In the rest home I found about fourteen officers, broken in health, seeking recuperation. I watched the ways and conversation of all most carefully, intending to confide in those who gave the best evidence of entire sanctification. There were some choice souls among them, and some arrogant hypocrites. But holiness in the absolute sense I saw in none. Some were very godly and devoted. Their conscientiousness I could not doubt. But those who talked the loudest were plainly the least spiritual. They seldom read their Bibles, they rarely conversed together of Christ. An air of carelessness pervaded the whole place. Three sisters, most devoted women, were apparently more godly than any others; but two of them admitted to me that they were not sure about being perfectly holy. The other one was non-committal, though seeking to help me. Some were positively quarrelsome and boorish, and this I could not reconcile with their profession of freedom from inbred sin. I attended the meetings held by the other workers I have mentioned. There the best of them did not teach sinless perfection; while the manifestly carnal gloried in their experience of perfect love! Sick people testified to being healed by faith, and sinning people declared they had the blessing of holiness! I was not helped, but hindered, by the inconsistency of it all.

At last I found myself becoming cold and cynical. Doubts as to everything assailed me like a legion of demons, and I became almost afraid to let my mind dwell on these things. For refuge I turned to secular literature, and sent for my books, which some years before I had foresworn on condition that God would give me the "second blessing." How little I realized the Jacob-spirit in all this! God seemed to have failed; so I took up my books once more, and tried to find solace in the beauties of essays and poetry, or the problems of history and science. I did not dare to confess to myself that I was literally an agnostic; yet for a month at least I could only answer, "I do not know" to every question based on divine revelation.

This was the legitimate result of the teaching I had been under. I reasoned that the Bible promised entire relief from indwelling sin to all who were wholly surrendered to the will of God. That I had thus surrendered seemed to me certain. Why then had I not been fully delivered from the carnal mind? It seemed to me that I had met every condition, and that God, on His part, had failed to perform what He had promised. I know it is wretched to write all this: but I see no other way to help others who are in the same state that I was in for that awful month.

Deliverance came at last in a most unexpected way. A lassie-lieutenant, a woman some ten years my senior in age, was brought to the Home from Rock Springs,

Wyoming, supposedly dying of consumption. From the first my heart went out to her in deep sympathy. To me she was a martyr, laying down her life for a needy world. I was much in her company, observed her closely, and finally came to the conclusion that she was the only wholly sanctified person in that place.

Imagine my surprise when, a few weeks after her arrival, she, with a companion, came to me one evening and begged me to read to her; remarking, "I hear you are always occupied with the things of the Lord, and I need your help." I, the one to help her! I was dumbfounded, knowing so well the plague of my own heart, and being fully assured as to her perfection in holiness. At the very moment they entered my room I was reading Byron's "Childe Harold." And I was supposed to be entirely devoted to the things of God! It struck me as weird and fantastic, rather than as a solemn farce--all this comparing ourselves with ourselves, only to be deluded every time.

I hastily thrust the book to one side, and wondered what to choose to read aloud. In God's providence a pamphlet caught my attention which my mother had given me some years before, but which I had dreaded to read lest it might upset me; so afraid had I been of anything that did not bear the Army or Holiness stamp. Moved by a sudden impulse, I drew it forth and said, "I'll read this. It is not in accordance with our teaching; but it may be interesting anyway."

I read page after page, paying little attention, only hoping to soothe and quiet this dying woman. In it the lost condition of all men by nature was emphasized. Redemption in Christ through His death was explained.

Then there was much as to the believer's two natures, and his eternal security, which to me seemed both ridiculous and absurd. The latter part was occupied with prophecy. Upon that we did not enter. I was startled after going over the first half of the book when Lieut. J-- exclaimed, "O Captain, do you think that can possibly be true? If I could only believe that, I could die in peace!"

Astonished beyond measure, I asked, "What! do you mean to say you could not die in peace as you are? You are justified and sanctified; you have an experience I have sought in vain for years; and are you troubled about dying?" "I am miserable," she replied, "and you mustn't say I am sanctified. I cannot get it. I have struggled for years, but I have not reached it yet. This is why I wanted to speak with you, for I felt so sure you had it and could help me!"

We looked at each other in amazement; and as the pathos and yet ludicrousness of it all burst upon us, I laughed deliriously, while she wept hysterically. Then I remember exclaiming, "Whatever is the matter with us all? No one on earth denies himself more for Christ's sake than we. We suffer, and starve, and wear ourselves out in the endeavor to do the will of God; yet after all we have no lasting peace. We are happy at times; we enjoy our meetings; but we are never certain as to what the end will be."

"Do you think," she asked, "that it is because we depend upon our own efforts too much? Can it be that we trust Christ to save us, but we think we have to keep saved by our own faithfulness--?"

"But," I broke in, "to think anything else would open the door to all kinds of sin!"

And so we talked till, wearied out, she arose to go, but asked if she and others might return the next evening to read and talk of these things we had gone over--a permission which was readily granted.

For both Lieut. J--and myself that evening's reading and exchange of confidences proved the beginning of our deliverance. We had frankly owned to one another, and to the third party present, that we were not sanctified. We now began to search the Scriptures earnestly for light and help. I threw all secular books to one side, determined to let nothing hinder the careful, prayerful study of the word of God. Little by little, the light began to dawn. We saw that we had been looking within for holiness, instead of without. We realized that the same grace that had saved us at first alone could carry us on. Dimly we apprehended that all for us must be in Christ, or we were without a ray of hope.

Many questions perplexed and troubled us. Much that we had believed we soon saw to be utterly opposed to the word of God. Much more we could not understand, so completely warped had our minds become through the training of years. In my perplexity I sought out a teacher of the Word who, I understood, was in fellowship with the writer of the pamphlet I have referred to above. I heard him with profit on two occasions, but still was in measure bewildered, though I began to feel solid ground beneath my feet once more. The great truth was getting a grip of me that holiness, perfect love, sanctification, and every other blessing, were mine in Christ from the moment I had believed, and mine forevermore, all because of pure grace. I had been looking at the wrong man--all was in another Man, and in that Man for me! But it took weeks to see this.

A booklet entitled Safety, Certainty, and Enjoyment proved helpful to both of us, and was a source of cheer. Other tracts were given me, and read with earnest purpose, looking up every reference, searching context and other passages of like, or apparently opposite, character, while daily we cried to God for the knowledge of His truth. Miss J--saw it ere I did. The light came when she realized that she was eternally linked with Christ as Head, and had eternal life in Him as the Vine, in her as the branch. Her joy knew no bounds, and she actually improved in health from that hour, and lived for six years after; finally going to be with the Lord, worn out in seeking to lead others to Christ. Many will be disappointed to know that she maintained her connection with the Army to the last. She had a mistaken (I believe) notion that she should remain where she was, and declare the truth she had learned. But ere she died she repented of this. Her last words to a brother (A.B.S.) and me, who were with her very near the end, were: "I have everything in Christ--of that I am sure. But I wish I had been more faithful as to the truth I learned about the Body--the Church. I was misled by zeal which I thought was of God, and it is too late to be faithful now!"

Four days after the truth burst upon her soul in that Home of Rest, I, too, had every doubt and fear removed, and found my all in Christ. To go on where I was, I could not. Within a week I was outside of the only human system I had ever been in as a Christian, and for many

28

years since I have known no head but Christ, no body but the Church which He purchased with His own blood. They have been happy years; and as I look back over all the way the Lord has led me, I can but praise Him for the matchless grace that gave me to see that perfect holiness and perfect love were to be found, not in me, but in Christ Jesus alone.

CAUSED HIM TO SET ME FREE FROM INTROSPECTION AND

And I have been learning all along my pilgrim journey that the more my heart is taken up with Christ, the more do I enjoy practical deliverance from sin's power, and the more do I realize what it is to have the love of God shed abroad in that heart by the Holy Spirit given to me, as the Earnest of the glory to come. I have found liberty and joy since being freed from bondage that I never thought it possible for a soul to know on earth, while I have a confidence in presenting this precious truth for the acceptance of others that contrasts with the uncertainty of the past.

THUS

ADD BLACK & WHITE PAGES HERE

PART II: DOCTRINAL

In commencing our inquiry on the subject of sanctification as taught in the Scriptures, it is of importance first of all that there be a clear understanding of the meaning which writer and reader attach to the word. For if the writer have one thought in his mind when he uses this expression, and the reader be thinking of something totally different as he peruses the treatise, it is not to be supposed that a common conclusion will ever be reached.

I propose, then, first of all, to let the theologians and the holiness teachers define the word for us; and then to turn To Scripture, there to test their definitions. Examples: "In a doctrinal sense sanctification is the making truly and perfectly holy what was before defiled and sinful. It is a progressive work of divine grace upon the soul justified by the love of Christ. The believer is gradually cleansed from the corruption of his nature, and is at length presented 'faultless before the presence of His glory with exceeding joy.' " This is a fair statement of the views held by ordinary Protestant theologians, and is taken from the Bible Dictionary edited by W. W. Rand, and published by the American Tract Society.

The secular dictionary definitions generally agree that "sanctification is an act of God's grace, whereby man's affections are purified and exalted." And this, it will be observed, practically accords with the definition already given.

Holiness writers are very explicit, and generally draw attention to what they suppose to be the difference between justification and sanctification. I shall not quote any of their authorities as to this, but put the teaching in my own language rather, as I often taught it in past years. My reason for this is that all holiness professors reading these pages may be able to judge for themselves as to whether I was "clear" as to the matter when numbered among them.

Justification, then, was supposed to be a work of grace by which sinners are made righteous and freed from their sinful habits when they come to Christ. But in the merely justified soul there remains a corrupt principle, an evil tree, or "a root of bitterness," which continually prompts to sin. If the believer obeys this impulse and wilfully sins, he ceases to be justified; therefore the desirability of its removal, that the likelihood of backsliding may be greatly lessened. The eradication of this sinful root is sanctification. It is therefore the cleansing of the nature from all inbred sin by the blood of Christ (applied through faith when a full consecration is made), and the refining fire of the Holy Spirit, who burns out all dross when all is laid upon the altar of sacrifice. This, and this only, is true sanctification—a distinct second work of grace, subsequent to justification, and without which that justification is very likely to be lost!

The correctness of the definition will, I think, be acknowledged by even the most radical of the "holiness" school.

Now let us test these statements by Scripture. And in order to do so intelligently, I purpose first to look at a number of passages in both Testaments, and see if in any of them either of the definitions given above would make good sense and sound doctrine. I would observe that holiness and sanctification are equivalent terms; both words being used to translate the one Greek or Hebrew noun. Twelve prominent examples may suffice to show how the term is used in our Bibles.

(1) The sanctification of inanimate objects is distinctly taught in the Word:

"Thou shalt anoint the altar of the burnt offering, and all his vessels, and sanctify the altar: and it shall be an altar most holy. And thou shalt anoint the laver and his foot, and sanctify it" (Ex. 40:10-11).

Are we to suppose any change took place in the nature of these vessels? Or was there any evil element rooted out of them?

Again, in Ex. 19:23 we read, "Set bounds about the mount [Sinai], and sanctify it." Was any change effected in the composition of the mountain when God gave the law upon it? Let the reader answer fairly and honestly, and he must confess that here at least neither the theological nor the "holiness" definitions apply to the word "sanctify." What it does mean we shall see later, when we have heard all of our twelve witnesses.

(2) People can sanctify themselves, without any act of divine power, or any work of grace taking place within them. "Let the priests also, which come near to the Lord, sanctify themselves" (Ex. 19:22). Were these priests then to change their own natures from evil to good, or to destroy from within themselves the principle of evil? Once more it is the readers' province to judge. I adduce the witnesses: they must be the jury.

(3) One man could sanctify another. "Sanctify unto Me all the first-born: . . . it is Mine" (Ex. 13:2); and, again, "The Lord said unto Moses, Go unto the people, and sanctify them; . . let them wash their clothes" (Ex. 19:10). What inward change, or cleansing, was Moses to perform in regard to the first-born, or the entire people of Israel? That he did not eliminate their inbred sin, the succeeding chapters amply testify.

(4) Persons can sanctify themselves to do iniquity. "They that sanctify themselves, and purify themselves in the gardens behind one tree in the midst, eating swine's flesh, and the abomination, and the mouse, shall be

consumed together, saith the Lord" (Isa. 66:17). How monstrous a sanctification was this, and how absurd the thought of any inward cleansing here!

(5) The Son was sanctified by the Father. "Say ye of Him whom the Father hath sanctified, and sent into the world, Thou blasphemest; because I said, I am the Son of God?" (John 10:36) They, not He, blasphemed: and equally vile would be the blasphemy of any who said that sanctification, for Christ, implied a corrupt nature eradicated, or a perverse will changed. He was ever "that Holy Thing . . . called the Son of God."

There are not wanting " holiness" advocates who impiously dare to teach that the taint of sin was in His being, and needed elimination; but they are rightfully refused fellowship, and their teaching abhorred by all Spirit-taught Christians. Yet He, the Holy One, was "sanctified by God the Father," as Jude writes of all believers. Are we to suppose the expression means one thing in relation to Christ, and quite another in regard to saints?

(6) The Lord Jesus sanctified Himself. "For their sakes I sanctify Myself, that they also might be sanctified through the truth" (John 17:19). If either of the definitions given above is to stand, then what are we to make of the fact that He who had been sanctified by the Father, yet afterward sanctified Himself? Is it not plain that there is some great discrepancy here between the theologians, the perfectionists, and the Bible?

(7) Unbelievers are sometimes sanctified. "For the unbelieving husband is sanctified by (in) the wife, and the unbelieving wife is sanctified by (in) the husband:

else were your children unclean; but now are they holy [or sanctified]" (1 Cor. 7:14). Here the life-partner of a Christian, though unsaved, is said to be sanctified. Is such a one, then, free from inbred sin, or undergoing a gradual change of nature? If this be too absurd for consideration, sanctification cannot mean either of the experiences specified.

(8) Carnal Christians are sanctified. "Paul, called an apostle of Jesus Christ, through the will of God, and Sosthenes our brother, unto the church of God which is at Corinth, to them that are sanctified in Christ Jesus" "I brethren, could not speak unto you as unto spiritual, but as unto carnal, even as unto babes in Christ. . . . For ye are yet carnal: for whereas there is among you envying, and strife, and divisions, are ye not carnal, and walk as men?" (1 Cor. 1:1, 2; 3:1, 3.) Carnal, and yet free from inbred sin? Impossible! Nevertheless they who are declared to be sanctified in chapter 1 are said to be carnal in chapter 3. By no possible system of logical reasoning can the class of the latter chapter be made out to be different from those addressed in the former.

(9) We are told to follow sanctification. "Follow peace with all men, and holiness [sanctification], without which no man shall see the Lord" (Heb. 12:14). In what sense could men follow a change of nature, or how follow the elimination of the carnal mind? I follow that which is before me—that to which I have not yet fully attained in a practical sense, as the apostle Paul tells us he did, in Phil. 3:13-16.

(10) Believers are called upon to sanctify God! "But sanctify the Lord God in your hearts: and be ready

always to give an answer to every man that asketh you a reason of the hope that is in you, with meekness and fear" (1 Pet. 3:15). How are we to understand an exhortation like this if sanctification implies an inward cleansing, or making holy what was before unclean and evil? Is it not manifest that such a definition would lead to the wildest vagaries and the grossest absurdities?

(11) Persons addressed as sanctified are afterward exhorted to be holy. "Peter, an apostle of Jesus Christ, to the strangers scattered throughout Pontus, Galatia, Cappadocia, Asia, and Bithynia, elect according to foreknowledge of God the Father, through sanctification of the Spirit, unto obedience and sprinkling of the blood of Jesus Christ. . . . As He which hath called you is holy, so be ye holy in all manner of conversation; because it is written, Be ye holy; for I am holy" (1 Peter 1:1, 2, 15, 16). Think of the incongruity here if sanctification and holiness refer to an inward work whereby inbred sin is rooted out of one's being! The sanctified are exhorted to be holy, in place of being informed that already they have been made absolutely that, and therefore need no such exhortation.

(12) The sanctified are nevertheless declared to be perfected forever. "For by one offering He hath forever perfected them that are sanctified" (Heb. 10:14). Who among the perfectionists can explain this satisfactorily? Nothing is commoner among the teachers of this school than the doctrine of the possibility of the ultimate falling away and final loss of those who have been justified, sanctified, and have enjoyed the most marvelous experiences; yet here the sanctified are said to be forever perfected—consequently shall never be lost, nor ever

lose that sanctification which they have once been the objects of.

After carefully hearing these twelve witnesses, I ask my readers, Can you possibly gather from these varied uses of the word "sanctification" any hint of a change of nature in the believer, or an elimination of evil implied therein? I feel certain that every candid mind must confess the word evidently has a very different meaning, and I design briefly to point out what that meaning is.

Freed from all theological accretions, the naked verb "to sanctify" means to set apart, and the noun "sanctification" means, literally, separation. This simple key will unlock every verse we have been considering, and bring all into harmony where discord seemed complete.

The vessels of the tabernacle were separated for divine service, even as mount Sinai was set apart to Jehovah for the giving of the law. The priests in Israel separated themselves from their defilement. Moses separated the people from uncleanness, and set apart the first-born as dedicated to Jehovah. The apostates in Isaiah's day set themselves apart, on the contrary, to work wickedness in the sight of the Lord. The Father set the Son apart to become the Saviour of the lost; and at the end of His life on earth, His work accomplished, the Lord Jesus separated Himself and ascended to glory, there to become the object of His people's hearts, that they might thus be set apart from the world that had refused and crucified their Redeemer. The unbelieving wife or husband, if linked with a saved life-partner set apart to God, is thereby put in an external relation to God, with its privileges and responsibility; and the children are likewise separated from those who never come under the sound of the truth. All Christians, whatever their actual state, be they carnal or spiritual, are nevertheless separated to God in Christ Jesus; and from this springs the responsibility to live for Him. This separation is to be followed daily, the believer seeking to become more and more conformed to Christ. Persons professing to be Christians and not following sanctification, will not see the Lord; for they are unreal, and have no divine life. The Lord God must be set apart in our hearts if our testimony is to count for His glory. One may be set apart to God in Christ, and yet need exhortations to a practical separation from all uncleanness and worldliness. And, lastly, all so set apart are in God's sight perfected forever, as to the conscience, by the one sacrifice of Christ on the cross; for they are accepted in the Beloved, and eternally linked up with Him. Get the key, and every difficulty vanishes. Sanctification, in the Christian sense, is therefore twofold—absolute and progressive.

SANCTIFICATION BY THE HOLY SPIRIT:

INTERNAL

In closing the last chapter I remarked that sanctification is both absolute and progressive. Absolute sanctification is by the one offering of Christ on the cross, and will be treated of further on. Progressive sanctification is looked at in two ways; it is by the Spirit and by the Word.

It may help some to put it this way:

Sanctification by the Spirit is INTERNAL. It is an experience within the believer.

Sanctification by the blood of Christ is ETERNAL. It is not an experience; it is positional; it has to do with the new place in God's eternal favor occupied by every believer—an unchanging and unchangeable position, to which defilement can never attach, in God's estimation.

Sanctification by the Word of God refers to the believer's outward walk and ways. It is the manifest result of sanctification by the Spirit, and goes on progressively all through life.

I desire to group together four scriptures which refer to the first important aspect above mentioned. Doctrinally, perhaps, I should take up sanctification by blood first; but experimentally the Spirit's work precedes the knowledge of the other.

In 1 Cor. 6:9, 10 we read of a host of sinful characters who shall not inherit the kingdom of God. The 11th verse immediately adds, "And such were some of you: but ye are washed, but ye are sanctified, but ye are justified, in the name of the Lord Jesus, and by the Spirit of our God."

Again, in 2 Thess. 2:13 we read, "But we are bound to give thanks always to God for you, brethren beloved of the Lord, because God hath from the beginning chosen you to salvation through sanctification of the Spirit and belief of the truth."

Closely linked with this is the second verse of the opening chapter of 1 Peter: "Elect according to the foreknowledge of God the Father, through sanctification of the Spirit, unto obedience and sprinkling of the blood of Jesus Christ."

The fourth verse is Rom. 15:16: "That I should be the minister of Jesus Christ to the Gentiles, ministering the gospel of God, that the offering up of the Gentiles might be acceptable, being sanctified by the Holy Ghost."

In all these passages it is of the utmost importance, in order to rightly apprehend the truth intended to be conveyed, to observe that sanctification by the Spirit is treated as the first beginnings of God's work in the souls of men, leading to the full knowledge of justification through faith in the blood-sprinkling of Jesus Christ.

Far from being "the second blessing," subsequent to justification, it is a work apart from which none ever would be saved. That this may be made plain to the thoughtful reader, I purpose a careful analysis of each verse quoted.

The Corinthians had been characterized by the common sins of men. They had, like the Ephesians (chap. 2:1-5), "walked according to the course of this age," lured on by that unholy "spirit that now worketh in the sons of disobedience." But a great change had taken place in them. Old affections and desires had been superseded by new and holy longings. The wicked life had been exchanged for one in which the pursuit after godliness was characteristic. What had wrought this change? Three expressions are used to convey the fullness of it. They had been "washed, sanctified, and justified"—and all "in the name of the Lord Jesus and by the Spirit of our God." Objective and subjective are here closely linked together. The work and character of the Lord Jesus had been presented as set forth in the gospel. He alone was the Saviour of sinners. But in the application of that salvation to men there is necessarily the subjective side. Men are unclean because of sin, and must be "washed." The "washing of water by the word" (of Eph. 5:25, 26) is clearly alluded to. The word of God lays hold on the conscience, and men are awakened to see the folly and wickedness of their lives—away from God, and walking in darkness. This is the beginning of a moral washing that goes on all through the believer's life, and of which I hope to treat more fully later on.

But now, observe carefully—the same word of God comes to all men, but the same effect is not produced in all. Christ and His cross is preached to an audience of a hundred unconverted men. One remains, broken-hearted over his sins and seeking peace with God, while ninety and nine go away untouched. Why the difference? The Holy Spirit gives power to the Word, plowing up the conscience in the case of every one truly converted, and such a one is separated, set apart by a divine work within, from the indifferent multitude to which he once belonged. It is here that sanctification of the Spirit applies. It may be some time ere he finds true peace with God; but he is never again a careless sinner. The Holy Spirit has laid hold of him for salvation. This is beautifully illustrated in the first few verses of our Bibles. The world created in perfection (see Isa. 45:18) in verse 1, is described as fallen into a chaotic condition in verse 2. "Without form and void," and covered with a mantle of darkness: what a picture of fallen man away from God! His soul a moral chaos, his understanding darkened, his mind and conscience defiled, he is in very deed dead in trespasses and sins; "alienated and an enemy in his mind by wicked works." All this the ruined earth may well speak of.

But God is going to remake that world. It shall yet become a dwelling-place for man, a fit home for him during the ages of time. How does He go about it? The first great agent is the Spirit; the second, the Word. "The Spirit of God moved [or brooded] upon the waters." Hovering over that scene of desolation, the Holy Spirit brooded; and then the Word of power went forth. "God said, Let light be: and light was." And so in the salvation of fallen man—the Spirit and the Word must act. The brooding-time comes first. The Holy Spirit quickens through the message proclaimed. He awakens men, and gives them a desire to know Christ and to be delivered from sin's power and saved from its judgment. After this brooding season, or as a result of it, the heart is opened to the gospel in its fullness; and, being believed, the light shines in and the darkness is dissipated. "God, who commanded the light to shine out of darkness, hath shined in our hearts, to give the light of the knowledge of the glory of God in the face of Jesus Christ" (2 Cor. 4:6). Thus are we who believe no longer children of the night, nor of darkness, but of the day. We were once darkness: now we have become light in the Lord. But ere the shining forth of the light there was the Spirit's brooding. And this is the sanctification referred to in the four passages grouped together above. Notice the order in 2 Thess. 2: "Chosen to salvation through sanctification of the Spirit"—the divine agency—"and belief of the truth"—the Word of life scattering the darkness and bringing in the light of the knowledge of salvation through the name of the Lord Jesus.

It is the same in 1 Peter. The saved are select, but it is the sanctification of the Spirit that brings them unto the obedience and blood-sprinkling of Jesus Christ. Now the knowledge of justification is mine when brought by the Spirit to the knowledge of the sprinkled blood of Jesus. It is faith apprehending that His precious blood cleanseth my soul from every stain, Thus giving peace. By the Spirit I am brought to this, and to begin a life of obedience—to obey as Christ obeyed. This is the practical effect of the Spirit's sanctification.

But now it is of importance to realize that justification is not in itself a state. It is not a work in the soul, but a work done by Another for me, yet altogether outside of me, and utterly apart from my frames and feelings. In other words, it is my standing, not my experience.

The difference between the two may be illustrated thus: Two men are haled into court charged with the joint commission of a crime. After a full investigation, the judge on the bench justifies them both. They are free. One man, hearing the decision, is filled with delight. He had feared an opposite verdict, and dreaded the consequences. But now he happy, because he knows he is cleared. The other man was even more anxious and gloomy. So occupied is he with his troubled thoughts that he does not fully catch the declaration of the court, "Not guilty." He hears only the last word, and he is filled with dismay. He sees a loathsome prison rising before him, yet he knows he is innocent. He gives utterance to words of despair until with difficulty made to comprehend the true status of the case, when he too is filled with joy.

Now what had the actual justification of either man to do with his state, or experience? The one who heard and believed was happy. The one who misapprehended the decision was miserable; yet both were alike justified. Justification was not a work wrought in them. It was the judge's sentence in their favor. ~~And this is the judge's sentence in their favor~~. And this is ever what justification is, whether used in the Bible or in matters of every life. God justifies, or clears, the ungodly when they believe in the Lord Jesus who bore their condemnation on the cross. To confound this judicial act with the state of soul of the believer is only confusion.

"But," say one, "I do not feel justified!" Justification has nothing has nothing to do with feeling. The Question is, do you believe God is satisfied with His beloved Son as your substitute upon the cross, and do you receive Jesus as your substitute—your personal Saviour? If so, God says you are justified; and there is an end to it. He will not call back His words. Believing the gospel declaration, the soul has peace with God. Walking with God, there is joy and gladness, and victory over sin in a practical sense. But this is state, not standing.

The Holy Spirit who quickens and sanctifies at the beginning, leading to the knowledge of justification through faith in what God has said about the blood-sprinkling of Jesus Christ, abides now in every believer, to be the power for the new life, and thus for practical sanctification day by day.

In this way the offering-up of the Gentiles—poor aliens, heathen of all descriptions, strangers to the covenants of promise—is made acceptable to God, being sanctified by the Holy Spirit. He accompanies the preaching—the ministry of reconciliation—opening the heart to the truth, convincing of sin, of righteousness and judgment, and leading to personal faith in the Son of God.

I think it must now be plain to any who have carefully followed me thus far that in this aspect at least sanctification is wrongly designated as a "second blessing." It is, on the contrary, the beginning of the work of the Spirit in the soul, and goes on throughout the believer's life, reaching its consummation at the coming of the Lord, when the saved one, in his glorified, sinless body, will be presented faultless in the presence of God. And so Peter, after telling the Christians to whom he writes that they are sanctified by the Spirit, very properly proceeds to exhort them to be holy because he who has saved them is holy, and they are set to represent Him in this world.

So too Paul, after affirming the sanctification of the Thessalonians, yet prays that they may be sanctified wholly, which would be an absurdity if this were accomplished when first sanctified by the Spirit. "The very God of peace sanctify you wholly; and I pray God your whole spirit and soul and body be preserved blameless unto the coming of our Lord Jesus Christ. Faithful is he that calleth you, who also will do it" (1 Thess. 5:23, 24). There is no room for doubt as to the final result. Sanctification is God's work; and "I know that, whatsoever God doeth, it shall be forever" (Eccl. 3:14). "He who hath begun a good work in you will perform it until the day of Jesus Christ" (Phil 1:6).

When asked for scripture as to the term "the second blessing," the perfectionist will generally refer you to 2 Cor. 1:15. There Paul writes to the Corinthians (who, as declared several times over in his own epistle, were sanctified), and says, "In this confidence I was minded to come unto you before, that ye might have a second benefit." The margin reads, "a second blessing." From this simple expression, an amazing system has been deduced. It is taught that as a result of Paul's first visit to Corinth many had been justified. But as the carnal mind remained in them, they manifested it in various ways, for which he rebukes them in his first letter. Now he longs to get to them again, this time not so much to preach the gospel as to have some "holiness meetings," and get them sanctified!

An ingenious theory surely! But it all falls to the ground when the student of Scripture observes that the carnal saints of the 1st epistle were sanctified in Christ Jesus (chap. 1:2); had received the Spirit of God (chap. 2:12); were indwelt by that Spirit (chap. 3:16); and, as we have already noticed at some length, were "washed, sanctified

45

and justified in the name of the Lord Jesus, and by the Spirit of our God" (chap. 6).

What then was the second blessing Paul desired for them? To begin with, it was not the second blessing at all, but a second blessing. They had been blessed by his ministry among them on the first occasion, as they learned from his lips and saw manifested in his ways the truth of God. Like any true-hearted under-shepherd, he longs to visit them again, once more to minister among them, that they may receive blessing, or benefit, a second time. What could be simpler, if the mind were not confused by faulty teaching, leading to one's reading his thoughts into Scripture, instead of learning from it?

From the moment of their conversion, believers are "blessed with all spiritual blessings in heavenly places in Christ," and the Spirit is given to lead us into the good that is already ours. "All things are yours" was written, not to persons perfect in their ways, but to the very Corinthians whom we have been considering, and that before they received, through the apostle Paul, a second benefit.

SANCTIFICATION BY THE BLOOD OF CHRIST:

ETERNAL

The great theme of the epistle to the Hebrews is that aspect of sanctification which has been designated positional, or absolute; not now a work wrought in the soul by the Holy Spirit, but the glorious results of that wondrous work accomplished by the Son of God when he offered up himself to put away sin upon the cross of Calvary. By virtue of that sacrifice the believer is forever set apart to God, his conscience purged, and he himself transformed from an unclean sinner into a holy worshiper, linked up in an abiding relationship with the Lord Jesus Christ; for "both He that sanctifieth and they who are sanctified are all of one: for which cause He is not ashamed to call them brethren" (Heb. 2:11). According to 1 Cor. 1:30, they are "in Christ Jesus, who of God is made unto us . . . sanctification." They are "accepted in the Beloved." God sees them in Him, and looks at them as He looks at His son. "As He is, so are we in this world" (1 John 4:17). This is not our state. No believer has ever been wholly like the Lord Jesus in a practical way. The highest and best experience would not reach up to this. But as to our standing (our new position), we are reckoned by God to be "as He is."

The basis of all this is the blood-shedding and blood-sprinkling of our Saviour. "Jesus also, that He might sanctify the people with His own blood, suffered without the gate" (Heb. 13:12). By no other means could we be purged from our sins and set apart to God.

The main argument of the epistle is very fully developed in chapters 8 to 10, inclusive. There the two covenants are contrasted. The old covenant asked of man what it never got—that is perfect obedience; because it was not in man to give it. The new covenant guarantees all blessing through the work of Another; and from the knowledge of this springs the desire to obey on the part of the object of such grace.

In the old dispensation there was a sanctuary of an earthly order; and connected with it were ordinances of a carnal character, which nevertheless foreshadowed good things to come—the very blessings we are now privileged to enter into the enjoyment of.

But in the tabernacle God had shut Himself away from sinful man, and He dwelt in the holiest of all. Man was shut out. Once only every year a representative man, the high priest, went in to God, "but not without blood." Every great day of atonement the same ritual service was performed; but all the sacrifices offered under the law could not put away one sin, or "make him that did the service perfect as pertaining to the conscience."

The perfection of Hebrews, let it be noted, is not perfection of character or of experience, but perfection as the conscience. That is, the great question taken up is, How can a polluted sinner with a defiled conscience, procure a conscience that no longer accuses him, but now permits him unhinderedly to approach God? The blood of bulls and of goats cannot effect this. Legal works cannot procure so precious a boon. The proof of it is manifest in Israel's history, for the continual sacrifices proved that no sacrifice sufficient to purge the conscience had yet been offered. "For then would they not have ceased to be offered? Because that the worshipers once purged should have had no more conscience of sins" (chap. 10:2).

How little do holiness professors enter into words like these! "Once purged!" "No more conscience of sins!" What do such expressions mean? Something, dear reader, which, if but grasped by Christians generally, would free them from all their questionings, doubts, and fears.

The legal sacrifices were not great enough in value to atone for sin. This having been fully attested, Christ Himself came to do the will of God, as it was written in the volume of the book. Doing that will meant for Him going down into death and pouring out His blood for our salvation: "By the which will we are sanctified through the offering of the body of Jesus Christ once for all" (10:10). Observe, then, that our sanctification and His one offering stand or fall together. We believe the record, and God declares "we are sanctified." There is no growth, no progress, and certainly no second work, in this. It is a great fact, true of all Christians. And this sanctification is eternal in character, because our great Priest's work is done perfectly, and is never to be repeated, as the following verses insist: "For by one offering He hath perfected forever them that are sanctified" (ver. 14). Could words be plainer or language more expressive? He who doubts shows himself either unwilling or afraid to rest on so startling a truth!

That one true sacrifice effectually purges the conscience once and for all, so that the intelligent believer can now rejoice in the assurance that he is forever cleansed from his guilt and defilement by the blood-sprinkling of Jesus Christ. Thus, and thus only, the sanctified are perfected forever, as regards the conscience.

A simple illustration may help any who still have difficulty as to this expression, peculiar to Hebrews, "a purged conscience." A man is in debt to another who has again and again demanded payment. Being unable to pay, and that because he has unwisely wasted his substance, and this known to his creditor, he becomes unhappy when in the latter's presence. A desire to avoid him springs up and takes control of him. His conscience is uneasy and defiled. He knows well he is blameworthy, yet he is incapable of righting matters. But another appears, who, on the debtor's behalf, settles the claim in the fullest manner, and hands to the troubled one a receipt for all. Is he now afraid to meet the other? Does he shrink from facing him? Not at all; and why? Because he has now a perfect, or a purged, conscience in regard to the matter that once exercised him.

It is thus that the work of the Lord Jesus has met all God's righteous claims against the sinner; and the believer, resting upon the divine testimony as to the value of that work, is purged by the blood of Christ and "perfected forever" in the sight of the Holy One. He is sanctified by that blood, and that for eternity.

Having been turned from the power of Satan unto God, he has the forgiveness of sins, and is assured of an inheritance among them that are sanctified by faith that is in Christ Jesus (Acts 26:18).

But there is an expression used farther on in the chapter that may still perplex and bewilder those who have not apprehended that profession is one thing, and possession another. In order to be clear as to this, it will be necessary to examine the whole passage, which I therefore quote in full, italicizing the expression referred to. "For if we sin wilfully after that we have received the knowledge of the truth, there remaineth no more sacrifice for sins, but a certain fearful looking for of judgment and fiery indignation which shall devour the adversaries. He that despised Moses' law died without mercy under two or three witnesses: of how much sorer punishment, suppose ye, shall he be thought worthy who hath trodden under foot the Son of God, and hath counted the blood of the covenant, wherewith he was sanctified, an unholy thing, and hath done despite unto the Spirit of grace? (vers. 26-29).

In what we have already gone over we have seen that ~~hath seen that~~ he who is sanctified by the one offering of ~~Christ upon who is sanctified by the one offering of~~ Christ upon the cross, ~~upon the cross~~, that is, by His precious blood, is perfected forever. But in this passage it is equally plain that one whom counts the blood of the covenant, wherewith he was sanctified, an unholy thing, shall be forever lost. In order not to miss the true force of this for our souls, it is necessary that we give some attention to what we have already designated "positional sanctification." Of old all the people of Israel, and all who were associated with them, were set apart to God both on the night of the passover and afterwards in the wilderness. But this did not necessarily imply a work of the Spirit in their souls. Many were doubtless in the blood-sprinkled houses that solemn night, when the destroying angel passed through to smite the unsheltered first-born, who had no real faith in God. Yet they were by the blood of the Lamb put in a place of blessing, a position where they shared in many hallowed privileges. So afterward with those who were under the cloud and passed through the sea, being baptized unto Moses in the cloud and in the sea. All were in the same position. All shared the same outward blessings. But the wilderness was the place of testing, and soon proved who were real and who were not.

At the present time God has no special nation, to be allied to which is to come into a position of outward nearness to Him. But He has a people who have been redeemed to Himself out of all kindreds and tongues and peoples and nations, by the precious blood of the Lamb of God. All who ally themselves by profession with that company are outwardly among the blood-sheltered: In this sense they are sanctified by the blood of the covenant. That blood stands for Christianity, which in its very essence is the proclamation of salvation through Christ's atoning death. To take the Christian place therefore is like entering the blood-sprinkled house. All who are real, who have judged themselves before God, and truly confided in His grace, will remain in that house. If any go out, it proves their unreality, and such can find no other sacrifice for sins; for all the typical offerings are done away in Christ. These are they of whom the apostle John speaks so solemnly: "They went out from us, but they were not of us; for if they had been of us, they would have continued with us: but they went out that they might be made manifest that they were not all of us" (1 John 2:19). These unreal ones were positionally sanctified; but as they were ever bereft of

52

faith in the soul, they "went out," and thus did despite to the Spirit of grace, and counted the blood of the covenant, wherewith they were sanctified, an unholy thing. These sin wilfully, not in the sense of failing to walk uprightly merely, but as utterly abjuring, or apostatizing from, Christianity, after having become conversant with the glorious message it brings to lost men.

But where it is otherwise, and the soul is really resting on Christ, positional sanctification becomes eternal: because the sanctified and the Sanctifier are, as we have seen, linked up together by an indissoluble bond. Christ Himself is made unto them wisdom, and this in a threefold way: He is their righteousness, their sanctification, and their redemption.

Here is holiness! Here is an unassailable righteousness! Here is acceptance with God. "Ye are complete in Him," through daily needing to humble oneself because of failure. It is not my practical sanctification that gives me title to a place among the saints in light. It is the glorious fact that Christ has died and redeemed me to God. His blood has cleansed me from all, or every, sin; and I now have life in Him, a new life, with which guilt can never be connected. I am in Him that is true. He is my sanctification, and represents me before God, even as of old the high priest bore upon his mitre the words "Holiness unto the Lord," and upon his shoulders and his heart the names of all the tribes of Israel. He represented them all in the holy place. He was typically their sanctification. If he was accepted of God, so were they. The people were seen in the priest. And of our ever- living High Priest we may well sing:

"For us He wears the Mitre
Where holiness shines bright;
For us His robes are whiter
Than heaven's unsullied light."

That there should be a life of corresponding devotedness and separation to God on our part no Spirit-taught believer will for a moment deny, as we will now consider.

SANCTIFICATION BY THE WORD OF GOD:

EXTERNAL RESULTS

In His great high-priestly prayer of the 17th of John, our Lord says of men given to Him by the Father, "They are not of the world, even as I am not of the world. Sanctify them through Thy truth: Thy word is truth. As Thou hast sent Me into the world, *EVEN SO HAVE I ALSO SENT THEM INTO THE WORLD.* And for their sakes I sanctify Myself, that they also might be sanctified through the truth" (vers. 16-19). This precious passage may well introduce for us the subject of practical sanctification—the ordering aright of our external ways, and bringing all into accord with the revealed will of God. At the outset we shall do well if we get it fixed in our mind that this is very closely related to that sanctification of the Spirit to which our attention has already been directed. The Spirit works within us. The Word, which is without us, is nevertheless the medium used to do the work within. But I have purposely dwelt separately upon the two aspects in order to bring the clearer before our minds the distinction between the Spirit's sanctification in us, which is the very beginning of God's work in our souls, and the application of the Word thereafter to our outward ways. New birth is our introduction into God's family; but although born again, we may be dark as to many things, and need the light of the Word to clear our bewildered minds. But through the sanctification of the Spirit we are brought to the blood of sprinkling: we apprehend that Christ's atoning death alone avails for our sins. We are sanctified by the blood of Christ, and able to appreciate our new position before God. It is now that in its true sense the walk of faith begins, and thereafter we need daily that sanctification by the truth, or the word of God, spoken of by our Lord.

It is evident that in the very nature of things this cannot be what some have ignorantly called "a second definite work of grace." It is, on the contrary, a life—a progressive work ever going on, and which ever must go on, until I have passed out of the scene in which I need daily instruction as to my ways, which the word of God alone can give. If sanctification in its practical sense be by the Word, I shall never be wholly sanctified, in this aspect of it, until I know that Word perfectly, and am violating it in no particular. And that will never be true here upon earth. Here I ever need to feed upon that Word, to understand it better, to learn more fully its meaning; and as I learn from it the mind of God, I am called daily to judge in myself all that is contrary to the increased light I receive, and to yield to-day a fuller obedience than yesterday. Thus am I sanctified by the truth.

For this very purpose the Lord has sanctified or set Himself apart. He has gone up to heaven, there to watch over His own, to be our High Priest with God in view of our weakness, and our Advocate with the Father in view of our sins. He is there too as the object of our hearts. We are called now to run our race with patience, looking unto Jesus, with the Holy Spirit within us and the Word in our hands, to be a lamp to our feet and a light to our path. As we value it, and are controlled by its precious truth made good to us in the Spirit's power, we are sanctified by God the Father and by our Lord Jesus Himself. For in the 17th of John He makes request of the Father, "Sanctify them through Thy truth." In Eph. 5:25-

26 we read, "Christ loved the Church, and gave Himself for it; that He might sanctify and cleanse it with the washing of the water by the Word." Here it is Christ who is the sanctifier, for He could ever say, "I and the Father are one." Here, as in John, sanctification is plainly progressive; and, indeed, that waterwashing of Ephesians is beautifully illustrated in an earlier chapter of John—the 13th. There we have our Lord, in the full consciousness of His eternal Sonship, taking the place of a girded servant to wash His disciples' feet. Washing the feet is indicative of cleansing the ways; and the whole passage is a symbolical picture of the work in which He has been engaged ever since ascending to heaven. He has been keeping the feet of His saints by cleansing them from the defilement of the way—those earth-stains which are so readily contracted by sandaled pilgrim-feet pressing along this world's highways.

He says to each of us, as to Peter, "If I wash thee not, thou hast no part with Me." Part in Him we have on the ground of His atoning work and as a result of the life He gives. Part with Him, or daily communion, is only ours as sanctified by the water of the Word.

That the whole scene was allegorical is evident by His words to Peter, "What I do thou knowest not now, but thou shalt know hereafter." Literal feet-washing Peter knew and understood. Spiritual feet-washing he learned when restored by the Lord after his lamentable fall. Then he entered into the meaning of the words, "He that is bathed* needeth not save to wash his feet, but is clean every whit." The meaning is not hard to grasp. Every believer is bathed once for all in the "bath of regeneration" (Titus 3:5, literal rendering). That bathing is never repeated. None born of God can ever perish, for all such have a life that is eternal, and consequently non-forfeitable (John 10:27-29). If they fail and sin, they do not need to be saved over again. That would mean, to be bathed once more. But he that is bathed needs not to have it all done again because his feet get defiled. He washes them and is clean.✳[As many now know, this word means a complete bath, and differs from the word used later for "wash" in the same verse.]

So it is with Christians. We have been regenerated once, and never shall be a second time. But every time we fail we need to judge ourselves by the Word, that we may be cleansed as to our ways; and where we daily give that Word its rightful place in our lives, we shall be kept from defilement and enabled to enjoy unclouded communion with our Lord and Saviour. "Wherewithal," asks the psalmist, "shall a young man cleanse his way?" And the answer is, "By taking heed thereto according to Thy Word."

How necessary it is then to search the Scriptures, and to obey them unquestioningly, in order that we may be sanctified by the truth! Yet what indifference is often found among professors of a "second blessing" as to this very thing! What ignorance of the Scriptures, and what fancied superiority to them, is frequently manifested! -- and that coupled with a profession of holiness in the flesh!

In 1 Thess 4:3 there is a passage which, divorced from its context, is often considered decisive as proving that it is possible for believers to attain to a state of absolute freedom from inbred sin in this world: "This is the will of

58

God, even your sanctification." Who can deny my title to perfect holiness if sanctification means that, and it is God's will for me? Surely none. But already we have seen that sanctification never means that, and in the present text least of all. Read the entire first eight verses, forming a complete paragraph, and see for yourself. The subject is personal purity. The sanctification spoken of is keeping the body from unclean practices, and the mind from lasciviousness.

Grossest immorality was connected with, and even formed part of idolatrous worship. The Greek mythology had deified the passions of fallen man; and these Thessalonian Christians had but just "turned to God from idols, to serve the living and true God." Hence the special need of this exhortation to saints newly converted, and who were living among those who shamelessly practiced all these things. But think of calling for this upon men freed from inbred sin! And the saints, as God's temple are to be characterized by a clean life, not by a life polluted by fleshly lusts.

Another aspect of this practical sanctification is brought before us in 2 Tim 2:19-22. We might call it ecclesiastical sanctification; for it has in view the faithful believer's stand in a day when corruption has come in among professing Christians, and the church as a whole, viewed in its character as the house of God, has fallen, and become as a great house in which good and evil are all mixed up together. It is a matter of most solemn import that, whereas here and elsewhere in Scripture he who would walk with God is called to separate himself from unholy associations and the fellowship of the mixed multitude, even though it be found in what calls itself the Church, yet there are large numbers, who testify to "living without sin," who nevertheless are united in church (and often other forms of) fellowship with unbelievers and professing Christians who are unholy in walk and unsound as to the faith. For the sake of such it will be well to examine the passage in detail.

The apostle has been directing Timothy's attention to the evidences of increasing apostasy. He warns against striving about words (verse 14), profane and vain babblings (verse 16); and points out two men, Hymenaeus and Philetus, in verse 17, who have given themselves over to these unholy speculations, and have thereby, through accepted by many as Christian teachers, overthrown the faith of some. And this is but the beginning, as the next chapter shows, for "evil men and seducers shall wax worse and worse, deceiving and being deceived" (3:13).

Now I apprehend that the first verse of chapter 3 follows verse 18 of chapter 2 in an orderly, connected manner. The apostle sees in Hymenaeus and Philetus the beginning of the awful harvest of iniquity soon to nearly smother everything that is of God. Go on with these men, listen to them, fellowship them, endorse them in any way, and you will soon lose all ability to discern between good and evil, to "take forth the precious from the vile."

But ere depicting the full character of the rapidly encroaching conditions, Timothy is given a word for his encouragement, and instruction as to his own path when things reach a state where it is impossible longer to purge out the evil from the visible church.

"Nevertheless the foundation of God standeth sure, having this seal, The Lord knoweth them that are His. And Let every one that nameth the name of the Lord* depart from iniquity" (or, lawlessness) (verse 19). Here is faith's encouragement, and here too is the responsibility of faithfulness. Faith says, "Let the evil rise as high as it may—let lawlessness abound, and the love of many wax cold—let all that seemed to be of God in the earth be swallowed up in the apostasy—nevertheless God's firm foundation stands, for Christ has declared, 'Upon this rock I will build My Assembly, and the gates of Hades shall not prevail against it"!

But this brings in responsibility. I am not to go on with the evil—protesting, perhaps, but fellowshipping it still—though it be in a reserved, halfhearted way. I am called to separate from it. In so doing I may seem to be separating from dear children of God and beloved servants of Christ. But this is necessary if they do not judge the apostate condition.

To make clear my responsibility an illustration is given in verse 20: "But in a great house there are not only vessels of gold and silver, but also of wood and of earth; and some to honor, and some to dishonor." The "great house" is Christendom in its present condition, where good and evil, saved and lost, holy and unholy, are all mixed up together. In 1 Tim 3:15 we read of "the house of God, which is the Church of the living God, the pillar and ground of the truth." This is what the Church should ever have been. But, alas, it soon drifted away from so blessed an ideal, and became like a great man's house in which are found all kinds of vessels, composed of very different materials, and for very different uses. There are golden and silver vessels for use in the dinning-room; and there are vessels of wood and earth, used in the kitchen and other parts of the house, often allowed to become exceedingly filthy, and at best to be kept at a distance from the valuable, and easily scratched or polluted, plate up-stairs.

"If a man therefore purge himself from these, he shall be a vessel unto honor, sanctified, and meet for the Master's use, and prepared unto every good work" (verse 21). The parable is here applied. The vessels are seen to be persons. And just as valuable plate might stand uncleansed and dirty with a lot of kitchen utensils waiting to be washed, and then carefully separated from the vessels for baser uses, so Timothy (and every other truly exercised soul) is called upon to take a place apart, to "purge out himself" from the mixed conditions, that he may be in very deed "a vessel unto honor, sanctified, and meet for the Master's use, prepared unto every good work."

Unquestionably this sanctification is very different from the Spirit's work in the soul at the beginning, or the effect of the work of Christ on the cross, by which we are set apart to God eternally. It is a practical thing, relating to the question of our associations as Christians. Let me follow out the illustration a step further, and I think all will be plain.

The master of the great house brings home a friend. He wishes to serve him with a refreshing drink. He goes to the sideboard looking for a silver goblet, but there is none to be seen. A servant is called, and inquiry made. Ah, the goblets are down in the kitchen waiting to be washed and separated from the rest of the household vessels. He is indignantly dispatched to procure one, and soon returns with a vessel purged out from the unclean collection below; and thus separated and cleansed it is meet for the use of the master.

And so it is with the man of God who has thus purged himself out from what is opposed to the truth and the holiness of God. He is sanctified, or separated, and in this way becomes "meet for the Master's use."

Of course it is not enough to stop with separation. To do so would make one a Pharisee of the most disgusting type; as has, alas, often been the case. But he who has separated from the evil is now commanded to "flee also youthful lusts: but follow righteousness, Faith, love, peace, with them that call on the Lord out of a pure heart." To do this, what need there is of the daily application of the word of God, in the spirit's power, to all our ways!

And this, as we have seen, is true feet-washing. Through the Word we are made clean at new birth. "Now are ye clean through the word which I have spoken unto you" (John 15:3). That Word is likened to water because of its purifying and refreshing effect upon the one who submits to it. In it I find instruction as to every detail of the walk of faith. It shows me how I am called to behave in the family, in the church, and in the world. If I obey it the defilement is washed out of my life; even as the application of water cleanses my body from material pollution.

Never shall I attain so exalted a state or experience upon earth that I can honestly say: Now I am wholly sanctified;

I no longer need the Word to cleanse me. As long as I am in this scene I am called to "Follow peace with all men, and holiness (or, sanctification), without which no man shall see the Lord" (Heb. 12:14). This one passage, rightly understood, cuts up by the roots the entire perfectionist theory; yet no verse is more frequently quoted, or rather misquoted, in holiness meetings!

Observe carefully what is here commanded: We are to follow two things: Peace with all men, and holiness. He who does not follow these will never see the Lord. But we do not follow that to which we have attained. Who has attained to peace with all men? How many have to cry with the psalmist, "I am for peace: but when I speak, they are for war"! (Ps. 120:7). And who have attained to holiness in the full sense? Not you, dear reader, nor I; for "in many things we all offend" (James 3:2). But every real believer, every truly converted soul, every one who has received the Spirit of adoption, does follow holiness, and longs for the time when, at the coming again of our Lord Jesus Christ, "He shall charge these bodies of our humiliation," and make them like "the body of His glory." Then we shall have reached our goal: then we shall have become absolutely and forever holy.

And so when the apostle writes to the Thessalonians, in view of that glorious event, he says: "Abstain from all appearance (every form) of evil. And the very God of peace sanctify you wholly; and I pray God your whole spirit and soul and body be preserved blameless unto the coming of our Lord Jesus Christ. Faithful is He that calleth you, who also will do it" (1 Thess. 5:22-24). This will be the glad consummation for all who here on earth, as strangers and pilgrims, follow peace and holiness,

64

and thus manifest the divine nature and the fruits of the Spirit.

But so long as they remain in the wilderness of this world they will need daily recourse to the laver of water—the cleansing word of God—which of old stood midway between the altar and the holy place. When all are gathered Home in heaven the water will no longer be needed to free from defilement ~~will no longer be needed to free from defilement.~~ In that scene of holiness therefore there is no laver; but before the throne John saw a sea of glass, clear as crystal, upon which the redeem~~ing~~ [ED] were standing, their ~~trolls~~ [TRIALS] and their ~~g~~ warfare over.

So throughout eternity we shall rest upon the word of God as a crystal sea, no longer needed for our sanctification, for we shall be presented faultless in the presence of His glory with exceeding joy.

> "Then we shall be where we would be;
> Then we shall be what we should be:
> ~~Then~~ [THINGS] that are not now, nor could be,
> Then shall be our ~~owe~~ [OWN]."

RELATIVE SANCTIFICATION

Nothing more clearly establishes the proposition we have been insisting on throughout—that sanctification is not the eradication of our sinful nature—than the way the word is used relatively, where it is positively certain there is no work of any sort contemplated as having taken place in the soul of the sanctified. Having carefully considered the absolute and practical aspects of sanctification, without which all profession is unreal, it may now be profitable to weigh what God has to say of this merely outward, or relative, holiness.

Already, in the chapter on sanctification by blood, we have seen that a person may in a certain sense be sanctified by association and yet all the time be unreal, only to become an apostate at last.

It is also true that in another sense people are said to be sanctified by association who are the subjects of earnest, prayerful yearning, and may yet—and in all probability will—be truly saved. But they are sanctified before this, and in view of it.

The seventh chapter of 1 Corinthians is the passage which must now occupy us. It contains the fullest instruction as to the marriage relation that we have in the Bible. Beginning with verse 10, we read, "And unto the married I command, yet not I, but the Lord, let not the wife depart from her husband: but and if she depart, let her remain unmarried, or be reconciled to her husband: and let not the husband put away his wife." As to this, the Lord had already given explicit instruction, as recorded in Matt. 19:1-12.

But owing to the spread of the gospel among the heathen of the gentiles a condition had arisen in many places which the words of the Lord did not seem fully to meet, having been spoken, as they were, ~~to meet, having been spoken, as they were,~~ to the people of the Jews, separated as a whole to Jehovah. The question that soon began to agitate the Church was this: Suppose a case (and there were many such) where a heathen wife is converted to God but her husband remains an unclean idolater, or vice versa: can the Christian partner remain in the marriage relationship with the unconverted spouse and not be defiled? To a Jew the very thought of such a condition was an offense. In the days of Ezra and Nehemiah certain of the returned remnant had taken wives of the surrounding mixed nations, and the result was confusion. "~~There~~ their children spake half in the speech of Ashdod, and could not speak in the Jews' language, but according to the language of each people" (Neh. 13:24). This state of things was abhorrent to the Godly leaders, who did not rest until all the strange wives had been put away, and with them the children, who were considered likewise unclean, and a menace to the purity of Israel.

With only the Old Testament in their hands, who could have wondered at it, if some zealous, well-meaning legalists from Jerusalem had gone like firebrands through the Gentile assemblies preaching a crusade against all contamination of this kind, and breaking up households on every hand, counseling converted husbands to cast out their heathen wives and disown their children as the product of an unclean relationship, and urging Christian wives to flee from the embraces of idolatrous husbands, and, at whatever cost to the affections, to forsake their offspring, as a supreme sacrifice to the God of holiness?

It was to prevent just such a state of affairs that the verses that follow those we have already considered were penned by inspiration of the God of all grace. Concerning this anomalous state the Lord had not spoken, as the time had not come to do so. Therefore Paul writes: "But to the rest speak I, not the Lord: If any brother hath a wife that believeth not, and she be pleased to dwell with him, let him not put her away. And the woman which hath a husband that believeth not, and if he be pleased to dwell with her, let her not leave him. For the unbelieving husband is sanctified by the wife, and the unbelieving wife is sanctified by the husband: else were your children unclean; but now are they holy [or, sanctified]. But if the unbelieving depart, let him depart. A brother or a sister is not under bondage in such cases: but God hath called us to peace. For what knowest thou, O wife, whether thou shalt save thy husband? or how knowest thou, O man, whether thou shalt save thy wife?" (vers. 12-16).

What an example have we here of the transcendent power of grace! Under law the unclean partner defiled the sanctified one. Under grace the one whom God has saved sanctifies the unclean.

The family is a divine institution, older than the nations, older than Israel, older than the Church. What is here, and elsewhere in Scripture, clearly indicates that it is the will of God to save His people as households. He would not do violence to the ties of nature which He Himself has created. If he saves a man who is head of a household, He thereby indicates that for the entire family He has blessing in store. This does not touch individual responsibility. Salvation, it is ever true, is "not of blood"; but it is, generally speaking, God's thought to deliver His people's households with themselves. So he declares that the salvation of one parent sanctifies the other, and the children too are sanctified.

Is it that any change has taken place within these persons? Not at all. They may still be utterly unregenerate, loving only their evil ways, despising the grace and fearing not the judgment of God. But they are nevertheless sanctified!

How does this agree with the perfectionists' view of sanctification? As it is evident the word here cannot mean an inward cleansing, his system falls to the ground. The fact is, he has attached an arbitrary meaning to it, which is etymologically incorrect, Scriptural untrue, and experimentally false.

In the case now occupying us the sanctification is clearly and wholly relative. The position of the rest of the family is changed by the conversion of one parent. That is no longer a heathen home in God's sight, but a Christian one. That household no longer dwells in the darkness, but in the light. Do not misunderstand me here. I am not speaking of light and darkness as implying spiritual capacity or incapacity. I am referring to outward responsibility.

In a heathen home all is darkness; there is no light shining whatever. But let one parent of that family be converted to God; what then? At once a candlestick is set up in that house which, whether they will or no, enlightens every other member. They are put in a place of privilege and responsibility to which they have been strangers hitherto. And all this with no work of God, as yet, in their souls, but simply in view of such a work. For the conversion of that one parent was God's way of announcing His gracious desires for the whole family; even as in the jailer's case He caused His servants to declare, "Believe on the Lord Jesus Christ, and thou shalt be saved, and thy house." The last few words do not guarantee salvation to the household, but they at once fix upon the jailer's heart the fact that the same way is open for the salvation of his house as for himself, and that God would have him count upon Him for this. They were sanctified the moment he believed, and soon rejoicing filled the whole house, when all responded to the grace proclaimed. [I desire heartily to commend here an excellent work on this subject by the late beloved C.H. Macintosh, "Thou and Thy House."]

This, then, is, in brief, the teaching of Holy Scripture as to relative sanctification—a theme often overlooked or ignored, but of deep solemnity and importance to Christian members of families of whom some ARE still unsaved. "What knowest thou, O wife, whether thou shalt save thy husband? Or how Knowest thou, O man, whether thou shalt save thy wife?" Labor on; pray on; live Christ before the rest from day to day, knowing that through you God has sanctified them, and is waiting to save them when they see their need and trust His grace.

I cannot pursue this theme more at length here, as to do so would divert attention from the main theme that is before us; but I trust that the most simple and uninstructed of my readers can now perceive that sanctification and sinlessness must in the very nature of the case be opposing terms.

And with this paper I bring to an end my examination of the use of the actual term sanctification in Scripture. But this by no means exhausts the subject. There are other terms still to be examined, the meaning of which the perfectionists consider to be synonymous with it, and to teach their favorite theory of the entire destruction of the carnal mind in the sanctified. These will be taken up, the Lord willing, in a few more papers in continuance.

Made in the USA
Columbia, SC
26 October 2023

24935333R00045